Saints in Street Clothes

Saints in Street Clothes

Building Sacred Neighborhoods
Where the Abandoned Become Beloved

By

Jarrod Dillon

Knights of Saint George Press

Knights of Saint George Press
Charleston, SC
Printed in the United States of America

ISBN: 979-8-9992359-4-7 (Print)

Cover design, interior layout, and typesetting: Knights of Saint George Press

For more information, visit: www.knightsofsaintgeorgepress.com

Printed in the USA

Introduction

There are books that inform, and then there are books that call you into battle. *This* is one of the latter.

What you are holding is not merely a collection of stories or a reflection on broken systems. It is a rallying cry. A roadmap. A declaration of holy war—not against people, but against despair, apathy, and the spiritual rot that has wormed its way into institutions meant to protect the most vulnerable. At its heart, this book is about **rescue**. It's about seeing what the world tries to hide: the suffering of children, the burnout of saints, the collapse of compassion—and choosing not to look away.

Fr. Jarrod Dillon has spent years walking the halls most of us pretend don't exist—residential treatment facilities filled with screaming, hopeless kids; CPS offices where children sleep on the floor; foster homes stretched to their breaking point. He has sat with boys whose fists speak before their words, girls who have been passed from stranger to stranger like paperwork, and exhausted caseworkers whose entire careers are lived behind locked doors and clipped budgets.

He has seen what happens when the system becomes the enemy. And he could not remain silent.

Fr. Jarrod's journey into this work began not as a social worker, not as a policy expert, but as a priest with a profound sense of vocation—a call to shepherd the lost, not only within the walls of the Church, but among the highways and back alleys where today's Good Samaritans are still needed. He understood that pastoral ministry could not be confined to Sunday liturgies or church programs. It had to follow Christ into the wounded places of the world—into the foster care crisis, into invisible homelessness, into the broken pipelines of trauma that stretch from childhood into incarceration.

The stories in these pages are real. The pain is real. But so is the hope. And it is this hope—this sacred refusal to give up—that led to the founding of the **Banner of Saint George**, a nonprofit born from Fr. Jarrod's vision.

The name itself tells you what kind of mission this is. Saint George, the martyr-saint and dragon-slayer, is a symbol not just of bravery but of spiritual defiance. According to tradition, George stood against a violent empire and a monstrous evil—and he did so armed with nothing but faith and the cross. The *banner* of Saint George is not a flag of conquest but of **protection**—a banner raised over the vulnerable, the orphaned, the forgotten. It is a signal to the world: these children are not abandoned. These families are not alone. There is still a Church that fights for them.

The Banner of Saint George nonprofit was formed to embody that fight. It is not another bureaucracy, not another vague promise of change. It is a blueprint for action. Its aim is simple and audacious: to build **a liturgical neighborhood**—a living, breathing community where foster families, children in crisis, social workers, and spiritual leaders are united in a common rhythm of prayer, healing, formation, and belonging.

At the center of that vision is **the Father Flanagan House**, the first spark of what Fr. Jarrod hopes will become a nationwide renewal. Inspired by the founder of Boys Town and other great Christian reformers, the Father Flanagan House isn't just a shelter —it's a **sanctuary**. It's a place where trauma is treated not like a diagnosis to be managed but like a wound to be healed. It's where children who have been told they are dangerous, disposable, or too far gone are met with stability, tenderness, and fierce protection.

Fr. Jarrod believes the future of foster care—indeed, the future of the Church—depends on **building communities that are intentionally liturgical**. That means more than just having a chapel on site. It means structuring life around prayer, meals, shared responsibilities, and deep, healing relationships. It means training and supporting foster families who know how to handle trauma and how to practice mercy, who are paid and equipped not like volunteers but like missionaries. It means embedding professional services—counselors, therapists, educators—into the life of the neighborhood itself, so that healing is not a visit but a way of life.

And it means telling a new story. That's what this book is: the story behind the mission. The heartbreaks that birthed it. The failures that shaped it. The holy rage that sustains it.

Each chapter pulls you deeper into the spiritual and human crisis at the heart of modern child welfare. It doesn't offer quick fixes. It doesn't romanticize the work. Instead, Fr. Jarrod lifts the veil. He shows us what we've been trained not to see: that children in the system are not statistics—they're souls. And the people trying to care for them—social workers, foster parents, church volunteers—are often saints burning out in silence.

But he also shows us that this can change.

He shares stories of resilience, of ordinary people doing extraordinary good, of little acts of faithfulness that point the way toward a more humane future. He outlines a practical vision: liturgical neighborhoods, wraparound support, deep formation, and a Church that refuses to let Caesar have the last word over children's lives.

At its core, *this book is about discipleship*. It's about the kind of radical discipleship that doesn't settle for charity when justice is required. That doesn't just host Christmas gift drives but opens its doors year-round. That doesn't just pray for children in crisis—but goes out to find them, to feed them, to parent them, to stand between them and the dragon.

The Banner of Saint George nonprofit is the vessel through which this discipleship takes flesh. It provides the legal, organizational, and pastoral structure to support the dream: to build neighborhoods rooted in the Gospel, where the traumatized are tended to, the workers are supported, and the Church is present not as a service provider but as a **family**.

Fr. Jarrod Dillon is not calling us to a trend. He's calling us to **a restoration**—a return to the Church's ancient vocation to defend the orphan, welcome the stranger, and bind up the wounded. His book is both a confession and a commission. It names our failures honestly—but also calls forth a new generation of foster saints, street priests, trauma-informed caregivers, and monastery builders who believe that the Kingdom of God looks like a table full of kids eating pancakes with someone who finally decided to stay.

If you've ever wondered what the Church should do in the face of overwhelming need—start here.

If you've ever felt a holy rage at how children are discarded in our culture—this is your book. If you've ever longed to build something better—read, and rise. Because this book is more than a collection of stories.

It's a battle plan.

And the banner has been raised.

6

Prologue

I'll never forget her voice.

She was nine years old, but she spoke like she was thirty. Her words were steady, measured—not childish or frantic, but soaked in sorrow and strange maturity. She wasn't supposed to be anyone's mother, yet there she was, trying to hold together a life unraveling in front of her. She was doing her best to be strong— for her siblings, for herself, and for the adults who kept making promises they couldn't keep.

She had just watched her father beat her mother so badly that she had to act. Her little hands turned violent. She kicked him in the back of the head to protect the woman who had given her life.

She told me this like it was a badge of honor. Like it proved she had done something right. And maybe it did. But what haunted me—what has never stopped haunting me—was the phrase she kept repeating:

"I just want to be strong for the kids."

She was a child herself. And yet she had already been pulled into the role of protector, caregiver, fighter, and witness. She had absorbed the chaos and made it her responsibility to shelter others from it. That phrase wasn't just something she said —it was something she had built a whole identity around. And I knew in that moment: this wasn't just her story. It was the story of thousands.

That was when it all shifted for me. That was the moment I knew I couldn't keep waiting for someone else to fix this.

It wasn't going to be the state.

It wasn't going to be a government agency.

It wasn't going to be the next election cycle or some reform package.

It had to be us.

It had to be me.

I've spent my life stepping into the aftermath of suffering —hospitals, hospices, prison wards, group homes, shelters, courtrooms, and makeshift placements in back offices where children fall asleep under fluorescent lights because there's nowhere else to go. I've seen how the system operates when it's doing its best—and I've seen how easily it falls apart.

And when it falls apart, children like her pay the price.

They don't just lose their families.

They lose their names.

They lose their voices.

They lose their sense of worth.

They become files. Numbers. A line in a case manager's spreadsheet. Their stories—so full of pain, complexity, and humanity—are reduced to diagnostic codes and risk factors. Every cry becomes a behavior. Every act of defiance becomes a liability. Every need becomes a burden. And slowly, silently, their personhood slips away.

But I have also seen the opposite.

I have seen grace show up—fierce, stubborn grace—right in the middle of the mess.

I've seen a tired, underpaid social worker pull into a drive-thru to buy Happy Meals for three hungry siblings, knowing it will come out of her own pocket, because there's no food in the office and no bed to place them in for the night.

I've seen a foster mom move into a bigger home—not because she needed more space, but because she refused to let two brothers be split apart and sent to different cities.

I've seen a man stay on the phone with his foster son for two straight hours while the boy punched, screamed, cursed, and fell apart. "He's just having a bad day," the man said afterward, his lip bleeding. And I believed him. Because love stays.

I've seen people like Brother Francis, who gave up everything—including his own rest—to keep one more soul from slipping through the cracks.

I've met saints in street clothes.

I've knelt at the tomb of Father Flanagan.

I've prayed with girls who cut themselves and boys who lash out—because violence is the only language of survival they've ever known.

I've listened to them scream. I've sat with them while they cried. I've heard them say things no child should know how to say. And I've made a decision.

We are going to build something better.

This isn't a book of theories. This isn't an abstract think-piece or a critique of bureaucracy. This is a battle plan. A blueprint. A cry from the heart and a call to arms.

We're going to build a home—a sacred space. A church. A school. A gym. A kitchen table. A neighborhood. A spiritual center where kids can be kids again. Where they can fall down and be picked up, fail and be forgiven, rage and be loved.

Where they can learn how to laugh again.

Where they can be called by name.

Where someone will look them in the eye and say, "You matter. You are not forgotten."

We're not going to create another institution.

We are going to build a family.

A communion of saints-in-the-making.

I've seen too many children locked away in sterile facilities, where no one knows their birthday and no one learns how to pronounce their name. I've been in rooms where people give up on thirteen-year-olds—labeling them "too damaged," "too far gone." I've worked in places that feel more like prisons than homes, where the staff turnover is faster than the trauma can be addressed, and no one lasts more than three days.

I've walked into rooms where the screaming never stops. Where hope is in short supply and love is even rarer.

And I've asked myself, again and again:

Why are we doing this?

Why are we failing?

Why aren't we loving them the way Christ commands?

This book is my response.

This plan. This dream. This house.

We are going to build something holy—not perfect, but holy. Something born in prayer, shaped by the liturgy, grounded in the Gospel. A place informed by the hard truths of trauma and the even harder truths of grace. A neighborhood where children can belong. Where the sacred and the practical come together in real ways. Where sacrifice isn't a slogan—it's the way we live.

We're going to build the Father Flanagan House—and from there, God willing, we will build a whole community. A village of healing. A place of real, stubborn hope.

We will staff it with people who know they aren't saviors but servants. With people who see children not as problems to be fixed, but as persons to be loved. With people who understand that holiness doesn't always look like halos—it often looks like holding someone's hand through a panic attack, or cleaning up after a breakdown, or staying in the room when everyone else has left.

Because I believe there is no such thing as a bad kid. Only kids who were never given a real chance.

And we're going to give them that chance.

We're going to kneel beside them.

We're going to walk with them.

We're going to train them, feed them, clothe them, pray for them, fight for them.

We're going to raise them—not as projects, not as charity cases, but as sons and daughters of God.

We're not promising it will be easy. Healing never is. Love, real love, always costs something. But if we fail—let it be said that we failed loving.

And honestly? I don't think we will.

Because I believe in them.

And I believe in you.

And I believe in the One who placed this burden on our hearts.

If you're holding this book, I believe God put it in your hands. Maybe you've seen what I've seen. Maybe you've felt the ache of watching the system swallow a child whole. Or maybe you've simply heard the whisper in your soul that says, You were made for more than watching.

Either way, you're part of this story now.

Because somewhere tonight, a nine-year-old girl is wrapping her arms around her little brother while their world falls apart. She's whispering into the dark:

"I just want to be strong for the kids."

It's time we got strong for her.

And built the kind of world she shouldn't have to imagine on her own.

Chapter One

When the System Becomes the Enemy

I met a boy once—thirteen years old, six-foot-three, and three hundred twenty pounds of muscle. His presence filled every room he entered. He was all rage and no hope, a walking furnace of pain. Beneath the surface, he was still just a child, but the world had long since stopped seeing him that way.

He lived in what the official forms called a "residential treatment facility." But let's stop pretending. Let's call it what it really was: a prison.

Not by name, of course. There were no razor-wire fences, no orange jumpsuits. But everything else was there—cameras posted on every wall, doors that only opened with keys, and staff trained more in restraint techniques than in compassion. There were cries at night, rooms that locked from the outside, and a sterile atmosphere that smelled of bleach and despair. A place where kids weren't healed—they were managed. Controlled. Contained.

We sat outside once, on a rusted picnic bench surrounded by chain-link and patchy grass. He asked to be as far from the building as they would let us go. "It's hell in there," he told me. His voice didn't crack. It wasn't dramatic. He was just telling the truth.

This boy had burned through foster homes like cheap light bulbs. One after another. A few were decent. One in particular stood out—a home run by a pastor and his wife. They gave him a Bible, told him about Jesus, tried to model kindness and structure. But when he acted out—and he did, often—they showed him the door. Like so many others, they didn't know what to do with a child raised by trauma.

It kept happening. Every new home promised stability, and every new home fell apart the moment he couldn't bottle up what he had carried since birth. He exploded. He fought. And when you're thirteen and built like an NFL lineman, adults stop seeing tantrums and start seeing threats. Nobody saw the brokenness anymore. Only danger.

He wasn't just angry. He was honest. He looked me in the eye and said, "Violence works. That's how the world is." He wasn't wrong. He had learned it fast—faster than most kids learn how to write cursive or solve fractions. The world had taught him that strength meant survival. That fists got results. That fear was currency.

Meanwhile, young social workers—fresh from college, full of idealism and theory—kept telling him, "Violence isn't the answer." But they were wrong, and he knew it. He had seen the world as it was, not as they imagined it should be. What they called dysfunction, he called survival. And instead of helping him turn that strength into something noble—into protection, defense, purpose—they told him to bury it. Suppress it. Deny the only thing that had ever kept him safe.

When I walked through that facility, I saw it with my own eyes—the chaos, the despair, the rawness of children living on the edge. I saw rooms that had been torn apart in rage. I saw kids so dysregulated they couldn't speak, only scream. I heard the stories: of teens jumping off rooftops to escape, of girls carving their arms open just to feel something, of staff members who shrugged and said, "We've lost control." I heard about one girl who cut herself so badly she nearly died. Another was assaulted. More than one tried to disappear.

And still, they called it "treatment."

I asked a few of the staff how long they'd worked there. "Four days," one said. Another: "Three." Not weeks. Days. This was a building full of traumatized, high-risk children—and the adults supervising them didn't even know their names.

There was no therapy happening. No real group work. No long-term healing plans. Just damage control.

And yet—I must say this—they meant well. Most of them did. The board members. The CEO. The program directors. They didn't want to hurt kids. They were trying. But the model they worked within was broken beyond repair. It was a holdover from another era, one that should've ended long ago. The state— terrified of liability—had only made things worse. In their effort to avoid scandal, they tied the hands of those still trying to care.

One incident had gone horribly wrong in another facility— something involving restraint—and now no one wanted to be the next headline. So the policy changed: no restraints, not even when safety demanded it. Not even when a child was harming themselves or others. Instead of reforming the system, they abandoned the kids inside it.

You know what the facility director told me? He looked me in the eye and said, "This is the worst it's ever been."

And that was enough.

I made the call. I asked the board to shut it down. To their credit, they did.

But that wasn't the end of the story.

Because when we closed the doors, those kids had nowhere to go.

The social workers—unsung heroes, most of them—scrambled to find placements. Unsafe placements. Emergency shelters. Motel rooms. Anywhere that would take them. I watched it unfold like a slow-motion disaster. Children—what I call AINTs: Abused. Isolated. Neglected. Traumatized.—shuffled like paperwork. Erased by red tape. Forgotten in files.

And I couldn't take it anymore.

So I started to dream.

Not of a better facility. Not of a more secure program.

I dreamed of a neighborhood.

A sacred neighborhood. A village built around worship and community. A church at the center. A school that understood trauma. A garden. A jiu-jitsu gym. A kitchen that always smelled like breakfast. A place where liturgy wasn't just for Sundays—it shaped the rhythm of life.

I dreamed of a place where children didn't get locked up—they got lifted up. Where foster families were equipped, not just licensed. Where autistic kids weren't punished for meltdowns—they were given tools and time. Where kids who had been abused weren't given more structure—they were given more belonging.

A place where you didn't have to be perfect to stay.

Where forgiveness was daily bread.

Where trauma wasn't a diagnosis—it was a wound that deserved gentleness.

Where every child was known by name.

That dream became the seed of something real: **The Father Flanagan House**.

It's not just a house—it's a signal fire. A lighthouse. A whisper to the world that things can be different.

And I'm not building it out of sentiment. I'm building it out of rage. Holy rage. The kind Jesus showed when He walked into the temple, flipped tables, and cried out, "You have made My Father's house a den of thieves." Because that's what we've done to these children. We've stolen their futures. We've monetized their pain. We've reduced sacred lives to statistics.

But it doesn't have to stay that way.

We can build something new. Not perfect. Not utopian. But holy.

A monastery for misfits. A refuge for the furious. A community rooted in prayer and pancakes, in sacraments and sweat. A neighborhood where bells ring and kids come running—not out of fear, but because they belong.

We can do this.

Because saints aren't born. They're formed.

And the ones God is calling now—the ones covered in scars, speaking in silence, acting out in rage—they're not broken beyond repair.

They are beloved.

The world may have given up on them.

But we haven't.

We won't.

Not ever.

Chapter Two

Invisible Homelessness

There are children sleeping in office buildings tonight.

That's not a metaphor. That's not exaggeration. That's reality. Actual kids—real, living, breathing, hurting kids—are curled up on the floors of CPS offices and government buildings, covered with thin blankets or jackets, resting their heads on backpacks, waiting for someone to find a place for them.

And no one talks about it.

Not because they don't care. Some of them care deeply. But most people just don't want to know. They don't ask. They look away. They assume someone else is handling it. They assume there's a plan in place. They assume "the system" is working.

Let me tell you the truth: the system is not working.

These kids don't show up in the public's imagination. They're not huddled in doorways on downtown streets. They're not sitting on freeway exit ramps with signs. They're not sleeping under bridges—at least, not yet. These kids are part of something we've come to call invisible homelessness.

They aren't counted in the usual numbers. They're not listed in HUD reports or captured in shelter tallies. They're not in obvious crisis locations, so they get missed. They sleep in cars. In friend's basements. In fast food booths until someone kicks them out. In emergency rooms. On couches. On the floor of an overwhelmed CPS worker's office. In makeshift motel placements, funded by emergency budgets.

They bounce between short-term spots—bounced by behavior, bounced by paperwork, bounced by panic. No continuity. No calm. No peace. They run because running feels safer than staying. And half the time, no one even knows where they are.

And when they do show up—bleary-eyed, anxious, half-starved from neglect—they're treated like liabilities. Like problems. Like broken things to be moved, not children to be embraced.

Let's be honest: some of them are scary. They've done scary things. They've broken property. Hurt others. Hurt themselves. Lit fires. Smashed windows. Run away. Screamed. Fought. Exploded.

But I've met them. I've sat with them. Listened to them.

And if you sit long enough, past the rage, past the cold stares and the threats, past the files full of infractions and diagnoses, you'll see it: a child who has been alone for too long.

A child who's had to raise themselves.

A child who was never given a second chance.

These kids are not evil. They are not monsters. They're not sociopaths or lost causes. They're unparented. They're abandoned. Not always in the literal sense—but emotionally, spiritually, practically.

People don't understand how little it takes to break a child. Not because they're weak, but because they're wired for love. For safety. For connection. Children are designed to develop within the shelter of a family. Not just to be fed and clothed, but to be known. To be seen. To be guided and loved and forgiven and taught.

Take those things away—strip them out—and the child will still survive. But they'll survive on instincts that aren't gentle. They'll learn control. Manipulation. Rage. Numbness. Violence. Whatever it takes to endure.

It becomes their armor.

I asked a kid once, "What's your earliest memory?"

He was quiet for a while. Then he said, "I was four. My mom left me on the porch. She said she was coming back. I waited until it got dark. Then I cried."

That was the moment his childhood ended. That's the origin story nobody writes down in his file. From that moment on, everything in his life was about survival—not development. Not joy. Not learning. Just getting through another night.

And then we dare to say he's "noncompliant."

We tell his story through police reports and discharge summaries. We label him "aggressive," "volatile," "too high risk." And we move him again. We write it up. We document the "incident." And somewhere in the notes, someone types, "He failed this placement."

No.

He didn't fail.

We did.

We failed to go back for him. We failed to build anything worthy of him. We created systems, protocols, and policies—but we never built what he really needed.

We didn't build family. We didn't build community. We didn't build a home.

And that's why I'm building the Father Flanagan House. That's why I won't shut up about invisible homelessness, even when people roll their eyes or change the subject. Because while politicians debate and departments shuffle budgets, kids are sleeping on tile floors with fluorescent lights humming overhead. And no one is coming for them.

I'm not interested in reforming another program. I'm not interested in improving metrics.

I want a neighborhood.

I want a bell tower that rings three times a day, not just to call people to prayer, but to say to every child, "You're still here. You still matter." I want homes rooted in hospitality and held together by prayer and meals and faithful presence. I want people who show up and stay, not because it's easy, but because it's holy.

I want foster families who aren't just "licensed," but who are called—trained, paid, and supported like the heroes they are. Not treated like temporary shelters or disposable providers. I want kids to be placed in homes where there's room to breathe, room to fail, room to grow.

I want them to be able to rage without being rejected.

I want them to be able to tell the truth without being branded.

I want staff who know their stories, not just their symptoms. Who can say, "You don't scare me. I know where this is coming from. And I'm not going anywhere."

I want a place that doesn't mistake surveillance for safety.

I want a porch light that stays on—every night—for the kid who's been running too long.

We've tried everything else.

And it hasn't worked.

So now we're going to try something radical.

We're going to love them.

We're going to train them.

We're going to stay with them when it's hard.

And when people ask, "What about accountability?" I'll ask in return: "What about ours?"

What about our accountability? What about our responsibility for the way we've failed these children? For the promises we never kept? For the dreams we let die?

Invisible homelessness doesn't end with a shelter.

It ends with a home.

It ends when a child who has slept in too many offices finds their name on a bedroom door.

It ends when the same person wakes them up every morning, and prays over them at night, and is still there the next day.

It ends when they know—really know—that they won't be moved again. That they are not a burden. That they are not disposable.

We are going to build that kind of home. One child at a time. One house at a time. One sacred neighborhood at a time.

Because that boy with the garbage bag?

That girl with the thousand-yard stare?

That child curled up under a desk in a government office?

They're not invisible to God.

And they won't be invisible to us.

Not anymore.

Chapter Three

Saints in Street Clothes

When people ask me what gives me hope in this work—when they ask how I stay in it, how I keep believing—it's not the politicians. It's not the grant writers. It's not the state contracts or the latest initiative with a trendy name.

It's the social workers.

It's the ones who stay.

You don't see them on TV. They don't get standing ovations. They don't have time to write memoirs or give TED Talks. But I've seen them walk into rooms that would paralyze most people and stay there. Stand there. Kneel there. Show up, again and again, for the sake of a child.

I've watched them pick up children after midnight, drive across the state in silence because the kid doesn't want to talk, stop at McDonald's on their own dime because the child hasn't eaten in twelve hours—and then do it again the next day. And the next.

They're underpaid. Exhausted. Misunderstood. Mocked by some. And absolutely holy.

I met one social worker who carried a caseload so large it would make your head spin. She had more children than hours in the week. And yet—she made every visit. She sent birthday cards. She showed up to court with her folders highlighted, color-coded, and tabbed. She cried in her car sometimes. Told me she was failing. But she wasn't. She was holding the whole thing together by sheer force of love.

These are the saints in street clothes.

Pope Francis once spoke of the "middle class of holiness"—not the canonized or the martyred, but the everyday people who don't call what they do "holy", though it is. That's who these people are. They don't wear collars. They don't stand behind pulpits. They aren't nonprofit CEOs. But they're the very heartbeat of compassion in a system barely holding together.

And I've met foster parents who should be canonized right now.

One woman adopted fifteen children with special needs. Fifteen. Not because she wanted attention. Not for the money. Not to be a hero. She simply couldn't bear the thought that they'd go unloved.

I met a dad who bought a bigger house just so two biological brothers wouldn't be separated. He didn't post about it. He didn't get a plaque. He just said, "It was the right thing to do."

I've visited a family who fostered teenagers no one else would touch. Teenagers with records, with rage, with deep trauma that scared off every other placement. When I asked why they did it, they shrugged and said, "We just wanted to give them a shot."

These are the real saints.

They are carrying the Church on their backs.

And they are burning out.

Because we haven't built anything around them. We commission them to fight fires and then hand them a paper cup. We send them into the battle with no reinforcements, and then we're surprised when they collapse. We whisper about their failures but ignore their faithfulness.

I've been inside these homes. I've sat at their kitchen tables, seen the fridge covered with therapy schedules and permission slips and crayon drawings. I've watched them juggle medical appointments, caseworker calls, school meetings, trauma meltdowns, and still manage to serve dinner.

I've watched them sit on the floor with a sobbing child, just holding space—just staying.

That's what makes a saint. Not a miracle. Not a vision. Not a halo. Just stubborn love. Relentless mercy. A refusal to give up, even when every part of you wants to.

But we've left them to starve spiritually, emotionally, even financially.

We treat foster parents like disposable resources. We pay them like part-time babysitters and expect them to function like full-time saints. Then we criticize them for needing help. We hold them to impossible standards while offering little more than lip service in return.

I've met social workers who have to choose which emergency gets their attention first. A suicidal teen threatening to jump? A newborn with no crib? A domestic abuse call that can't wait?

They triage trauma like ER doctors with no nurses. They go home to tiny apartments, exhausted, barely holding their own lives together—and still show up the next day, again and again.

That's not burnout. That's *sacrifice*.

And they aren't asking for much. They're not asking for praise. They're not asking for parades or headlines. They're asking for backup. For community. For someone to stand beside them and say, "We see you. We're with you. You're not alone."

That's why we're building the *Father Flanagan House*.

It's not just a neighborhood for kids. It's not just a project or a model. It's a sanctuary for saints.

A place where exhausted workers can find rest. Where weary foster families can breathe again. Where the people doing the hardest work in the world don't have to do it by themselves anymore.

We're going to surround foster parents with support—real support. Not just a phone number, but wraparound care. Professional help. Training. Counseling. Meals. Childcare. Pastoral presence. Friends.

We're going to wrap social workers in prayer and infrastructure, so they can do their job without crumbling. We're going to build spaces where grace isn't just an idea—it's the air you breathe.

Because sainthood isn't just for monasteries.

It's for minivans with stale coffee in the cupholder and half-crushed Goldfish crackers on the floor.

It's for the woman who buys a Happy Meal for a crying child because she doesn't know what else to do.

It's for the dad who takes a verbal lashing from a traumatized teenager and holds back tears, because he knows it's not really about him.

It's for the single foster mom who calls the caseworker in panic and says, "I don't know how to do this," and then gets up the next morning and does it anyway.

The saints I know don't wear robes. They wear hoodies. Scrubs. Pajama pants. They carry diaper bags and clipboards.

They sing lullabies in hospital rooms. They cry in court parking lots. They pray in whispered desperation and laugh whenever they get the rare moment to.

And if the Church cannot make room for them, cannot bless them, cannot "see" them—then the Church is failing.

But we can fix that.

We can build something new.

We can build a room in the house of God where these saints are not just remembered after death but honored while they live.

We can bake casseroles for them. We can sit with them through midnight tantrums. We can babysit their foster kids while they go to therapy. We can cover their bills. We can pray their names aloud during liturgy. We can show up. We can stay.

Because they're already here.

They're the hidden backbone of this entire calling.

They're the ones holding everything up.

And they're tired.

They need help.

They need us.

And I believe—with everything in me—that if the Church stands up, if the people of God stop looking away, we can change this. We can raise the arms of the weary. We can build something beautiful and hard and sacred.

We can build a liturgical neighborhood. A holy home. A living community where grace lives next to grit, where saints wear street clothes, and where no one carries the burden alone.

Because this isn't someone else's work. It's ours.

Let's build it.

Chapter Four

The Call to Boys Town

I didn't grow up knowing who Father Edward J. Flanagan was. His name wasn't in my schoolbooks. I didn't learn about him in seminary. He wasn't in the hagiographies I kept on my bookshelf or the litany of saints I prayed to as a boy. Honestly, I stumbled across his story like someone digging in the backyard and unexpectedly striking something solid—only to brush away the dirt and find a buried heirloom, something both beautiful and clearly meant to be passed down.

It started with a visit to Holy Cross Children's Services. At one time, it had been the largest private child welfare agency in all of Michigan. They had priests, brothers, and sisters. They had chapels and farmlands and workshops and dormitories. It was built on discipline, prayer, and the vision of the Church actually living among the poor—not just offering charity, but building community.

But when I arrived, it was a ghost town. It had unraveled under the weight of changing times. The buildings were still standing, but the soul had been stripped from them. The brothers were mostly gone. The chapel was quiet. You could feel what had once been—but only in the absences.

That's where I met Brother Chester.

He was old, gentle, and mostly quiet. He moved like someone carrying memories too heavy for words. He still believed in what the place had been. He spoke in a slow, reverent tone about what had been lost—not with bitterness, but with grief. He told me stories about a time when the Church didn't outsource its mission to government contracts. He remembered when prayer bells rang through the fields. When meals were sacred. When confession lines stretched out the chapel doors.

And it was Brother Chester who first spoke the name: "Father Flanagan."

I didn't know it yet, but that name would change my life.

I went home and started reading. I looked up everything I could find. Old quotes. Grainy black-and-white photos. Archived newsreels. I dug through Catholic history books and stumbled on stories that sounded more like legend than fact—except they were real. This was no ordinary man. Father Flanagan was a firebrand wrapped in a cassock. He didn't just grieve the brokenness of the world—he fought it. He didn't merely lament the condition of boys in prison—he took them out. Literally. He walked into juvenile jails, pointed at the children, and told the guards: "I'll take him. And him. And him."

And they let him.

Because somehow, even the courts believed him.

He saw what others didn't want to see: the Irish immigrant boys left to rot in institutions, the orphans labeled "incorrigible," the kids with disabilities written off by society, the violent boys no one dared to touch. He saw them all—and refused to call them bad. Instead, he gave them a home.

Not a facility. A home.

Not a program. A neighborhood.

He didn't ask for permission. He didn't wait for a committee. He didn't design a ten-year plan or wait for grant approval. He just did it. He bought a house. He found a cook. He brought the boys in. And when that house filled up, he built another. And another. And another. Until it was an entire village.

Boys Town.

It was an ecosystem of healing. There was a church at the center. A school. Farmland. Vocational training. Discipline rooted in dignity. Love that was neither soft nor sentimental—but rooted in respect and relentless consistency. The boys rose at the bell, worked the land, knelt in pews, learned carpentry, read books, served Mass. They were given expectations. They were given tools. But most of all, they were given family.

I had to see it.

So I made the pilgrimage to Boys Town.

And the moment I stepped onto that campus, I felt something I can only describe as holy residue. Like a current was still running under the surface. Like something sacred had soaked into the soil. The buildings still stood tall. The chapel rose like a sentinel in the center of the village. Everything radiated outward from that sanctuary: the gym, the homes, the school. It was not just designed for functionality. It was designed for formation.

It wasn't just a place to house boys. It was a place to form saints.

I sat in the pew where Father Flanagan once preached. I knelt where the boys had once confessed. I looked at the photos lining the halls—faces of young men who had been rescued, reborn, and released into the world not as threats, but as leaders. And I wept.

Not just because it was beautiful. But because I knew.

This was the blueprint.

This was the thing we'd been looking for in all our conferences and symposiums, buried beneath layers of bureaucracy and buzzwords.

This was the forgotten map.

We talk today about trauma-informed care. We talk about wraparound services, evidence-based models, cultural sensitivity, restorative justice, family preservation, and system reform.

But while we were busy perfecting our language, we lost our legacy.

Flanagan wasn't waiting for federal funding. He wasn't submitting white papers. He didn't have a TED Talk.

He had the Gospel.

He had a cassock, a vision, and a house full of boys everyone else had thrown away.

And he made saints out of them.

That's when it hit me: what if Boys Town wasn't just history? What if it wasn't a relic—but a seed? What if it didn't end with Father Flanagan? What if it was meant to begin again?

And what if I wasn't supposed to admire it from a distance —but to live it?

That's what led to the dream of the Father Flanagan House.

It's not just a home. It's not just a facility. It's not a rebranding of foster care. It's a resurrection. A return to the holy neighborhood.

A parish that raises children.

A gym that trains boys in discipline and virtue.

A kitchen table where forgiveness is passed around with the bread.

A school where scripture and poetry share the same blackboard.

A chapel that rings a bell three times a day and calls kids to remember they are not alone.

That's the dream. And it didn't come from me. It came from the voice of a man long dead but still speaking, saying: "There is no such thing as a bad boy."

I believe that. Not as sentiment. But as theology.

We don't build this for optics. We don't build it for applause. We build it because God became a child—and every child bears his image.

We are not looking for clients. We are raising brothers.

We are not checking boxes. We are breaking chains.

We are not managing trauma. We are redeeming lives.

And we won't do it perfectly. We will fall short. We'll be overwhelmed. But we will do it together—with the Church at the center, the Spirit as our guide, and Father Flanagan's legacy as our north star.

Because the neighborhood isn't gone.

It's just waiting to be built again. One house. One table. One prayer at a time.

And when the bell rings in the morning, it will ring for them.

And it will ring for him.

And it will ring for us all.

Chapter Five

How to Build a Neighborhood That Heals

We're not going to fix child welfare by rearranging paperwork. We're not going to fix it by rebranding old models or tweaking regulations from a state office. And we're certainly not going to fix it with more talk.

We're going to fix it by building neighborhoods.

I don't mean that metaphorically. I mean actual neighborhoods. Streets. Sidewalks. Gardens. Kitchens with tables where meals are shared. Houses that stay put. Schools where teachers know your name. A church where the doors are always unlocked. A chapel bell that rings every morning.

This isn't about programs. This is about place.

Children do not heal in systems. They heal in relationships. And relationships need space to breathe. They need roots. They need rhythm. They need permanence. They need a place where the child is not an emergency to be managed but a person to be formed.

When I started dreaming about the Father Flanagan House, I didn't want another facility. I wasn't interested in whiteboards and strategy plans. I didn't want to build an empire of intervention services. I wanted the beginning of a new world.

A holy world.

I wanted to build something beautiful enough to honor the pain these kids have carried. Something stable enough to hold their chaos. Something sacred enough to restore their sense of dignity. Something honest enough to tell the truth: you were not made for pain. You were made for joy. And it's not too late.

But we had to start from scratch.

No retrofits. No bureaucratic patchwork. No band-aids. We needed to pour new foundations—literally.

So here's the blueprint:

We begin with one house.

Just one. A small, simple home. It's led by a trained, supported foster family—a married couple or a single parent who doesn't see this as a side project but as a vocation. They're paid a real, living wage—not a stipend. Because sacrifice shouldn't mean starvation. They're backed up with real professionals—social workers, therapists, coaches, case managers, mentors—who know this family's name, who show up consistently, who pray with them, cry with them, laugh with them, and carry the load.

That's the first light on the street. That's the Father Flanagan House.

Then we build outward.

The Church comes next. Not a stage. Not a screen. Not a marketing strategy. A sanctuary. A real altar. A priest who lives nearby. The sacraments celebrated with reverence and joy. A place where Christ is encountered not in abstraction but in presence—body, blood, soul, and divinity. The liturgy becomes the rhythm of daily life. Morning prayer. Midday Angelus. Evening Vespers. Mass. Confession. The Rosary. Adoration. These are not burdens. They're oxygen.

The Church is not an accessory to the neighborhood. It is the beating heart.

From the sanctuary, everything else radiates.

Next comes **The School**. A place of learning, yes—but more importantly, a place of belonging. A place where trauma isn't punished but understood. Where teachers are trained to see behind the behavior. Where the classrooms are filled with grace and grit. Where every room has a prayer corner—and a punching bag. Because sometimes the Gospel is best preached through gentleness, and sometimes it needs to be lived out in movement and sweat. A school where failure is never final. Where a child can fall apart and still be invited back the next morning. Where Jesus is not a poster on the wall but the subject of every lesson.

Then we build **The Gym**. Yes, a gym. Because the body keeps score. Because trauma is not just psychological—it's physical. The nervous system remembers what the mind forgets. These kids need to move. They need jiu-jitsu. They need to lift weights. They need to hit something that won't hit back. They need to sweat, strain, stretch. Because sometimes formation of the soul begins with discipline of the body. A gym where a kid can learn to channel rage into respect, pain into perseverance, weakness into strength.

At the edge of the neighborhood is **The Garden**. This isn't just for food—it's for beauty. It's for watching something grow. Because many of these children have only ever seen things break. The garden is where they bury seeds and wait. Where they water life. Where they taste their own tomatoes and pick flowers for the chapel. Where they begin to believe that slow, quiet, ordinary miracles still happen.

And then, at the center of it all, we hang **The Bell**.

The chapel bell. It rings three times a day—morning, noon, and night. And every time it rings, the neighborhood pauses. Just for a moment. Just enough to breathe. To remember. To whisper a prayer. To know, "I am part of something. I am not alone."

This is not a treatment facility.

This is a neighborhood of healing.

This is what the Church used to build.

We forget that the Church once led the way. It built hospitals, orphanages, schools, shrines, monasteries, clinics, sanctuaries, and entire towns. We named them after saints and staffed them with the faithful. They weren't always perfect—but they were holy. They weren't run like corporations. They were lived like sacraments.

Somewhere along the line, we stopped.

We surrendered our imagination. We handed the work off to the state. We traded the radical for the reasonable. We tried to make ourselves efficient, compliant, and cost-effective. And in doing so, we forgot our roots.

We forgot that the Gospel isn't a program. It's a person.

And people need places.

Children don't need more protocols. They need permanence. They don't need more supervision—they need formation. They don't need better labels—they need love that stays.

The goal isn't innovation. It's incarnation.

We need to put skin back on the mission.

The neighborhood we build must be real—real walls, real gardens, real food, real laughter. It must be a place where a child with a garbage bag of clothes and a shattered history walks through the front door and sees something he's never seen before:

A family.

Not a perfect one.

But a permanent one.

A home that doesn't evict after the first meltdown. A community that doesn't abandon when it gets hard. A parish that celebrates their birthday even if no one else ever has. A neighbor who knows their favorite cereal. A priest who remembers their name in the Eucharistic prayer.

That might be the most radical thing we could offer: consistency.

A holy kind of stability.

And yes, it will be messy. There will be blowups and heartbreak. Things will break. People will get tired. But the neighborhood will still be there the next day. And the next. And the next.

Because the kids we're building this for—these "invisible" children—have been shuffled like paperwork for too long. They've been reduced to diagnoses. They've been managed, restrained, sedated, displaced, and forgotten.

No more.

We're going to build a place where they are not managed but mentored. Not contained but called. Not pitied but formed.

We will form saints.

Not soft, sanitized saints—but real ones. Saints with scars. Saints who know what it's like to rage and repent. Saints who've seen hell and still choose heaven. Saints who remember the day they heard the bell ring and realized: I belong.

This is not idealism. It is discipleship.

It is a return to the early Church. House to house. Bread to bread. Prayer to prayer.

It will take everything we've got.

And it will be worth it.

Because when a boy stands in the doorway and looks out at the chapel, the school, the gym, the garden, and hears the bell ringing in the distance—he'll know something unshakable:

This place was built for me.

This neighborhood is my home.

And no matter what happens—no matter how many nights he breaks down, no matter how many times he runs, no matter how deeply the pain resurfaces—he'll know he's still part of it.

He'll still belong.

Because we're not building an institution.

We're building a neighborhood.

And neighborhoods don't quit.

They ring the bell.

They make dinner.

They leave the porch light on.

And they wait for their children to come home.

Chapter Six

The Rhythm That Heals

The first thing the child hears in the morning is the bell.

It's not loud. It's not jarring. It doesn't scream like an alarm clock, commanding obedience with stress and panic. It rings like a heartbeat—steady, sacred. A pulse from the chapel that whispers, "You're not alone. The day has begun. And it's yours."

Not the system's.

Not the staff's.

Yours.

From that moment forward, the day unfolds—not as a schedule to be enforced, but as a rhythm to be lived. It's not institutional timekeeping. It's liturgical life. Like a monastery, like a family, like music.

Because trauma is chaos. It shatters time, it dissolves memory, it scrambles the senses. And the only thing that heals chaos is order—order rooted in love. Not the rigid control of punishment, but the peace that comes when you know what's coming next, when you know you'll still be safe tomorrow, when you know someone will still be there to wake you up.

At the Father Flanagan House, the day begins with prayer. Not mandatory. Not mechanical. Just gathered.

Someone lights a candle. Someone reads a psalm. The kids sit on couches with blankets or on the floor with sleepy eyes. Nobody's forced to speak. But everyone breathes. Everyone listens. A name is offered. A need. A thank you. Sometimes it's one word. Sometimes it's just the flame dancing in the silence. And that's enough.

Then comes breakfast.

Real breakfast. Not plastic-wrapped pastries or vending machine granola. Pancakes, eggs, fresh fruit. Toast with butter. Coffee for the adults. Cereal for the child who still flinches at the sight of steam. Grace before meals, spoken slowly, without irony. No phones at the table. No blaring TV. Just people—talking, chewing, laughing, or sitting in silence. All of it counts.

Because the point is not perfection.

The point is presence.

After breakfast, it's time for chores. Simple things. Sweeping. Making the bed. Wiping the table. Not as a punishment. Not as payment. But as participation. Because every child needs to contribute—not because they owe something but because they belong here. And belonging requires responsibility.

A child who is never invited to sweep the floor will never feel like it's his floor.

Some of the kids who arrive have been moved so often, they don't even unpack anymore. They live out of garbage bags or crumpled backpacks. They leave their socks in piles because they don't believe they'll be staying long enough to fold them.

So we teach them to unpack.

We teach them to plant their feet.

We give them drawers, name tags, a place to hang their coat. And we guard those details fiercely—because they are the scaffolding of safety. They are the signs that this is not just another placement. This is a home.

Then comes school.

But remember: this isn't a facility. It's a neighborhood.

The school is just down the street. Kids walk together. Staff greet them by name. Every adult is trained—not just in math or reading, but in trauma. They know what it means when a child zones out in class. They don't assume defiance. They ask better questions. They read the body before the behavior.

A child who punches a wall is not a threat. He's grieving.

A child who can't sit still is not "noncompliant." She's dysregulated.

A teenager who won't make eye contact might not be rude —he might just be afraid of being seen.

We teach academics, yes. We want our kids to thrive in reading, writing, science, and math. We want them to graduate, to dream, to apply to college if they want to. But more than that, we teach them that they are good. That their minds are not broken. That their trauma is not the end of their story. That learning is possible—and that it can be joyful.

And then, at noon, the bell rings again.

It's time for the Angelus.

The whole neighborhood pauses. It doesn't matter where you are. In the chapel, a small group gathers to pray. On the porch, a foster mom crosses herself. In the kitchen, someone stops stirring the soup and bows his head.

The rhythm continues. The holy is remembered. Time is reoriented. We are not running a race. We are walking with God.

After lunch, the day continues—school, homework, therapy, recess, sports, chores. But no matter what's happening, the pattern holds.

Every day, each child has some form of physical activity. Not to exhaust them. To empower them.

Through martial arts, team sports, dance, hiking, weightlifting—whatever fits the child—they learn something sacred: what their body can do. Not just what has been done to it.

They learn control. They learn strength. They learn to stretch instead of strike, to breathe instead of break. And slowly, the body begins to trust itself again.

Evening brings the rhythm's slow descent.

Dinner is shared again—at the table, with grace, with patience, with a few seconds of stillness before the meal begins. Sometimes the conversation is light. Sometimes it's heavy. Sometimes someone yells or cries or storms off. That's okay. The table stays set.

No one loses their seat for being human.

Some nights there's confession. Some nights Mass. Some nights a walk under the stars with a staff member who knows the child's story and knows how to be quiet with him.

And then, as the night deepens, the whole house gathers again for Compline—night prayer.

The lights dim. A candle is lit. The words are simple:

"Protect us, Lord, as we stay awake; watch over us as we sleep…"

Some kids fidget. Some kids weep. Some fall asleep on the couch. But the prayer is said. The peace is offered. The candle is blown out.

And a child who once slept curled up in the corner of a group home floor now lies in a bed with clean sheets, a nightlight, and maybe—even just maybe—a rosary in his hand.

Not every night. But some nights.

And that's enough.

Because healing doesn't happen in a single breakthrough moment.

It happens in rhythm.

Again and again and again.

Prayer. Meal. Work. Rest. Forgiveness. Repeat.

The world teaches traumatized children one thing: survive.

But survival is not the goal.

We teach them how to live.

Not reactively. Not defensively. Not fearfully.

But deeply. Joyfully. Together.

And slowly, the chaos that once defined their every breath begins to fade. It's replaced—not by silence—but by a different kind of sound:

The sound of a bell.

The clatter of plates.

The hum of a story being told.

The whisper of prayer over a tired child.

The slow breath of someone who finally feels safe enough to sleep.

This is not a miracle of efficiency. It's a miracle of rhythm.

A miracle of pattern, order, love, and time.

It doesn't look flashy. It doesn't raise capital easily. It won't trend on social media. But it works.

Because the rhythm that heals is older than every trauma.

Older than every wound.

It's the rhythm of the Church.

The rhythm of sacraments, of prayer hours, of candlelight, of meals shared with Christ.

It's the rhythm of a monastery, translated into a neighborhood.

And it's the rhythm we will never stop playing.

No matter how long it takes.

No matter how many days fall apart.

Because healing happens in rhythm.

And we are going to build a neighborhood that never forgets how to keep the beat.

Chapter Seven

Who Will Raise These Children?

You can't outsource love.

You can pay for therapy. You can fund programs. You can write policies and pass legislation. But you cannot mass-produce the kind of fierce, faithful love that heals a traumatized child.

That kind of love is incarnational. It has a name, a face, a voice that stays steady when the child is shaking with fear. It doesn't show up for a shift and leave at 5 p.m. It doesn't document behavior and walk away. It weeps. It stays. It doesn't run when the storm hits—it plants its feet deeper.

And the people who do that? They're not just parents. They're missionaries. They're saints-in-the-making.

At the Father Flanagan House, we're not just looking for foster families. We're calling people into vocation.

That means we're not recruiting warm bodies to fill open beds. We're not handing over broken children to unprepared caregivers and hoping for the best. We're forming people—spiritually, emotionally, and practically—to take on the hardest, holiest task in the world: raising children the world gave up on.

This is not a side hustle. This is not charity. This is a full-time, all-in, liturgically grounded, trauma-informed life. And it begins with one simple truth:

God is calling parents. Not perfect parents. Not saintly experts. But called parents. Ordinary people who are willing to do extraordinary things—not because they're strong enough, but because they've been summoned.

These parents must be trained—not just in CPR and licensing standards—but in the deeper work: how to see a meltdown as a message. How to interpret silence. How to hold a child through grief without fixing, without preaching, without judging, without running away.

So we create a formation process.

Ten weeks. Based in community. Structured like catechesis. Grounded in Scripture. Informed by neuroscience. Saturated in prayer. We don't just hand out information—we create transformation.

We start with their own story. Because if you don't know your own story, you will repeat it. Trauma unexamined becomes trauma reenacted. We ask every potential caregiver to look at their childhood, their wounds, their habits, their fears. Not to shame them—but to free them. To help them become aware. To help them become whole. A wounded caregiver who doesn't know they're wounded will transfer that pain to a child. But a caregiver who has faced their story with Christ becomes a healing vessel. And then we give them tools:

- **Attachment Theory and the Gospel.** How Jesus re-parents us and teaches us to re-parent others. His Incarnation wasn't just for theology—it was for re-humanizing the traumatized.

- **Regulation, not domination.** How to help a child calm their nervous system without coercion or control. How to be the thermostat in the room, not the thermometer.

- **Boundaries and mercy.** How to say "no" like a shepherd—not like a cop. How to discipline without shame. How to correct with dignity.
- **Daily liturgy.** How to let the rhythm of the Church shape the rhythm of the home. How morning prayer, table grace, evening Compline, and feast day celebrations anchor the chaos in sacred routine.
- **The Rosary and the Routine.** Because both matter. And both work. The rosary trains the soul in repetition and beauty. The routine trains the body in trust and predictability.
- **Crisis response.** What to do when everything goes wrong—and how not to take it personally. How to hold space, how to recover, how to stay.
- **Community life.** Because no one does this alone. Because isolation breeds burnout, and community sustains courage.

But we don't stop at training. We surround our foster families with spiritual support, professional coaching, and backup from people who've been through the fire. Every family is placed in a network—other foster families, mentors, intercessors, trauma therapists, and pastoral leaders who walk with them daily.

We tell them the truth: this will be the hardest thing you ever do.

But also the holiest.

Because in the moment when a child throws a chair across the room and screams at you, and you stay—that's the moment sainthood begins.

In the moment when a teenager tells you she hates you, and you say, "I still love you"—that's the moment you become the Church.

In the moment when a boy refuses to speak to you for days, and you keep making him toast anyway—that's the moment grace becomes incarnate.

We are forming what I call the **Spiritual Core**.

These are the people—parents, social workers, mentors, case aides, neighbors—who will become the heart of the neighborhood. They live by the sacraments. They pray like their life depends on it. They train like athletes. They confess. They rest. They refuse to quit.

And they need rest. Real rest.

So we give them **Sabbath**.

One day a week, each family gets rest. Not optional. Not "if you get time." Scheduled. They are relieved by a team—trained volunteers and staff—who come in and take over the house so they can breathe, pray, cry, sleep, go to a movie, visit family, or just be human again.

Because even saints need rest. Even Christ withdrew to quiet places. Even Moses needed Aaron to hold up his arms.

And we raise up **spiritual companions**—elders, pastors, counselors, and brothers—who walk with these families. No one ever gets left alone. If someone's struggling, they don't get scolded. They get surrounded. There is no punishment for burnout. There is only help.

Because in this neighborhood, failure is not exile. It's a call for reinforcements.

We also train the children.

Not in behavior charts. Not in shame. Not in compliance.
In **virtue**.

We call them to greatness. We teach them how to serve.
How to listen. How to set the table. How to pray. How to forgive.
How to fight for good. How to tell the truth. How to clean their
room not because they're afraid—but because it's their room.
We teach them that holiness is possible—even for them.

Especially for them.

We teach them to name their pain—but not to become it.

We teach them to see anger not as evil—but as a signal.

We teach them to feel fear—and choose courage anyway.

We teach them to pray even when they don't believe, to
trust even when they've been betrayed, to hope even when hope
has been taken from them again and again.

We invite them into the rhythm of the Church—not as an
obligation, but as a gift.

Because the question is not: Can we handle this?

The question is: Do we believe this is **sacred**?

If we do, we'll build the support structure.

If we do, we'll form the spiritual community.

If we do, we'll raise these children with the tenderness of
monks and the discipline of soldiers.

And we won't be afraid.

Because when God calls a community to raise saints, He
always provides what they need.

We just have to say yes.

We just have to remember that this is not a project.

This is a **mission**.

This is how the Church heals the world—one house, one parent, one child, one meal, one psalm, one nightlight at a time.

The real question is not "Who will raise these children?"

The real question is: **Who will answer the call?**

Chapter Eight

No Such Thing as a Bad Kid

There's a line that still echoes through my head every time I meet a new child in crisis:

"There is no such thing as a bad boy."

– Father Edward J. Flanagan

He said it in 1917 when most people were locking up the poor, orphaned, disabled, and delinquent. He said it when boys were being sentenced to life in institutions at age ten. He said it when the world had already given up.

And he said it because he knew something most people still don't:

Behavior is not identity.

We've built a whole child welfare system around the idea of fixing behavior. Correcting it. Managing it. Documenting it. Charting it. Confining it. We hold up data charts and incident reports like they tell the truth. But all they really show is the surface.   The smoke. The byproduct of the real thing burning underneath.

When a child punches a wall, we ask, "What's wrong with him?"

We should be asking, "What happened to him?"

When a child steals food, runs away, hoards snacks, lies about simple things, or lashes out—we often say they're manipulative. But maybe they're just surviving the only way they know how. Maybe every one of those behaviors is a form of armor, crafted over years of neglect, pain, and broken trust.

I met a boy once who was kicked out of four placements in two months. The file said "oppositional defiant." The staff said he was impossible. Therapists labeled him treatment-resistant.

But when I finally sat down with him—no clipboard, no checklist—he looked at me with tired, angry eyes and said, "No one ever keeps me."

That was it.

That was the truth. Not the diagnosis. Not the behavioral write-ups. That sentence: *"No one ever keeps me."*

We live in a world that expects broken children to behave as if they've been loved their whole lives. And when they don't—when they act out the pain that's been acted upon them—we treat them like problems to be managed instead of people to be loved.

So at the Father Flanagan House, we change the narrative.

We don't label kids by what they've done. We name them by who they are becoming.

We call them **SAINTS**.

Not as a gimmick. Not as flattery. As formation. As prophecy.

Because what we call a child has power.

We speak this identity over them daily—not as a wish but as a work. Not something they must achieve, but something they are being shaped into. Slowly. Messily. Truly.

We even break it down for them:

- **S – Safe and Supported**
  Because no healing happens outside of safety. Safety is the foundation of belonging, and support is the scaffold they can lean on until they can stand on their own.

- **A – Accountable and Affirmed**

  We do not ignore sin, and we do not ignore dignity. Children learn that they can be corrected without being crushed—and affirmed without being idolized.

- **I – Inspired by Christ**

  We introduce them to the One who never left them, even when everyone else did. The One who knows their pain. Who holds their wounds. Who still calls them by name.

- **N – Needed and Named**

  They are not burdens. They are necessary. They have something to give. We name them with hope. With belonging. With identity.

- **T – Trained in Truth**

  We disciple them in reality—not fantasy. We teach them about choices, about virtue, about resilience, about what it means to walk in the light.

- **S – Sent with a Mission**

  They are not just being "helped." They are being commissioned. Formed. Made ready to go and serve others, even in small ways. Even today.

We build this into everything—our prayers, our classrooms, our discipline, our dinner tables. We don't let them forget that they're not defined by their worst moment. They're defined by the God who made them and the family that refuses to give up on them.

But we're also honest.

Not every kid *feels* like a saint. Some feel like what I call an **AIN'T**—abused, isolated, neglected, and traumatized.

An AIN'T is a child who's been treated like trash for so long they start to believe it. They internalize the message: *I'm not lovable. I'm not wanted. I'm not safe.* And so they test you. They dare you to leave. They break things before you can.

Because that way, the rejection is at least on their terms.

The moment you try to love them, they push back harder. Because they don't trust good things. They've learned that good things leave. Or hurt. Or disappear.

And here's the secret: every AIN'T is just a **saint-in-waiting**. They are what the Church Fathers would call "the unformed image." The clay is still soft, but it hasn't been shaped by love yet. And what they need isn't more behavior charts or stricter punishment.

They need one thing: **Support.**

Sainthood isn't earned through performance. It's formed in the crucible of community—through love, structure, forgiveness, and a family that stays.

We've seen kids come in raging, broken, violent—and become protectors, builders, older brothers, spiritual leaders. Not because we "fixed" them, but because we believed in them. Again and again.

And that belief isn't abstract. It's embodied. It's in the meals we cook. The doors we don't slam. The apologies we give. The prayers we pray out loud, even when they're angry. It's in the clean socks folded at the foot of the bed. It's in the ride to school even after a meltdown. It's in the way we say, "Try again," instead of, "That's it."

That's the theological vision of the Father Flanagan House:

We are not saving kids.

We are **recognizing them**.

We are not "giving them purpose."

We are **uncovering what God has already placed within them**.

And we are **relentless** in that work.

Even when they run.

Even when they break things.

Even when they fail again.

Even when they throw our love back in our face.

We stay.

Because someone has to. Because somewhere along the way, the child starts to believe it too. They stop saying, "No one ever keeps me." They start saying, "I'm staying." They start helping the new kid unpack. They start praying. They start asking questions. They start brushing their teeth. They start forgiving. They start becoming the saint they were always meant to be.

And they do it slowly. Awkwardly. With relapses and regressions and bad days. But the trajectory bends. The seed begins to grow. The shell starts to crack.

You want to end the cycle? You want to stop generational trauma?

Start by naming the truth.

There are no bad kids.

Only children waiting to be seen. To be safe. To be named.

Start with that.

And stay.

Chapter Nine

The Sacrament Is the System

When people ask what makes the Father Flanagan House different, I don't begin with trauma-informed care, therapeutic homes, or community support—even though all of that matters and all of it is true. I say something simpler. More ancient. More powerful.

I say this: we are a **sacramental neighborhood**.

That means our way of life does not revolve around performance charts or management techniques. It does not begin with crisis response protocols or end with discharge plans. It revolves around **grace**—real grace. Tangible grace. Grace that touches the body, anchors the soul, and refuses to stay in the realm of theory.

Because if these children—some of whom have never known stability, who have been tossed from place to place like objects in a system built for liability rather than love—are going to believe that healing is possible, they need to **see** it. They need to **touch** it. **Smell** it. **Taste** it. **Hear** it ring like a chapel bell in the morning. They need to encounter God not in abstraction, but in **presence**. They need something that binds the invisible to the ground they walk on.

The state has systems. We have **sacraments**.

And in this neighborhood, the sacraments aren't an afterthought. They're not something we fit in on Sundays between appointments. They are not accessories to our mission. They **are** the mission. They are not the garnish. They are the meal.

They do not supplement the system. They **replace** it.

61

Let me show you how.

Baptism: The Name That Cannot Be Taken

Every child who enters the Father Flanagan House is reminded of their baptism. If they've never been baptized, we invite them—not with pressure, not as a requirement, but as a gift freely offered, a door gently opened. If they have been baptized, we help them remember it. We make it visible. We bless them with holy water when they come home at night. We keep the font flowing in the chapel like a spring that never dries up. And when the shame or the confusion begins to creep in, we say it out loud and without apology: **this is who you are**. Not your file. Not your past. Not your probation. You are not a burden. You are a child of God, sealed and claimed.

In a world that strips identity, **baptism gives it back**.

Confession: The Place Where Guilt Is Washed

Some of the teenagers come in ashamed of what they've done. Others show up still proud of it—wearing pain like armor, trying to prove they don't care. But eventually, in almost every case, there comes a moment when the weight hits them. Not the consequence. The guilt. The sorrow.

In the traditional model, the only answers are court dates or therapy sessions.

We add a third: **confession**.

A space where they kneel. Where they speak the truth. Where they hear words they never thought they'd be offered: **"You are forgiven."**

And something cracks. Something opens. Sometimes it starts with silence. Sometimes it ends in sobs. But it is real. The mercy is real. And the freedom that comes isn't theoretical—it's bodily. It's the moment a young man walks out of the chapel and doesn't need to perform anymore.

Not perfect. But not condemned.

And they begin to believe: **I am not what I've done**.

Eucharist: The Table That Cannot Be Broken

This is the center.

Every Sunday—and on many weekdays—we gather as a neighborhood around the altar. Not just the children. Everyone. The staff. The mentors. The volunteers. The priest. The neighbors. We gather as one body and lift up the bread and the wine and say together, "This is my Body... given for you."

And suddenly the hierarchy flattens. The abused and the abuser. The staff and the runaway. The social worker and the dropout. They kneel shoulder to shoulder. No one earns it. No one pays for it. Everyone receives it.

It is the meal that breaks down walls.

And the kids understand it. They know hunger. They know what it means to eat. They know what it feels like to sit at a table and not be wanted—and now they know what it feels like to be welcomed.

To be waited for.

To be fed.

The Eucharist becomes more than theology. It becomes safety. Family. Sacredness.

It becomes **home**.

Confirmation: The Call to Become Who You Are

We don't treat confirmation like a graduation. We don't rush it through to check a box. We wait.

We wait until they know what they're saying yes to. We wait until they've wrestled with the question of identity—not just faith, but **belonging**. And when the day comes, and they stand before the community, and we lay hands on their shoulders and anoint them with oil, we speak it clearly and without compromise:

You are not a mistake. You are not what your father did to you. You are not a file in a cabinet or a line item on a budget.

You are a warrior. You are a disciple. You are sealed.

We don't throw parties for high school diplomas. We throw them for confirmation.

Because that's the day they claim who they already are in the eyes of God.

Anointing of the Sick: Not Just for Dying

We use this sacrament more than most places.

Not because our kids are dying, but because so many of them are wounded. Deeply. And this sacrament is for the wounded.

We anoint them before court hearings. Before visits with a parent who might not show. Before their first therapy session or their fifth failed placement.

We anoint staff when they want to quit. We anoint their hands when they hold a child who's just relapsed. We anoint homes when a new child moves in. We anoint the doors and the beds and the tables where reconciliation happens.

Because we believe oil still heals.

And the Spirit still shows up.

We do not keep the sacraments locked behind rules and schedules. We bring them to the places where they are most needed.

To the wound. To the fear. To the moment when love feels furthest away.

Holy Matrimony and Holy Orders: The Vocations That Anchor the Neighborhood

Not every sacrament applies directly to the kids, but every sacrament is present.

The married couples who foster in our homes live out the sacrament of matrimony not just as romance or duty, but as a living witness to stability. To covenant. To fidelity. They model what it looks like to stay—especially when it's hard.

And the presence of priests, religious brothers, and consecrated men and women in our neighborhood means the call to Holy Orders is not abstract—it's visible. It walks the streets. It visits the kids. It anoints them and counsels them and eats dinner at the same table.

When a child sees a marriage that works or a priest who listens, they begin to imagine their own future in a different shape.

This is the difference.

Other models offer services.

We offer **sacraments**.

Other models manage behavior.

We invite **conversion**.

Other models reduce children to diagnoses.

We elevate them to **communicants**.

This isn't a program with a little liturgy on the side. It's not Catholic social work with a few prayers sprinkled in. It is a **parish**. A **community**. A **way of life** rooted in the oldest truth the Church has ever offered: that God came to us in the flesh, and still does.

The altar is not removed from the trauma. It stands in the center of it. It speaks directly to it. It answers it.

And when a child learns not just how to function, but how to **worship**, something changes. Not right away. Not magically. But deeply.

They stop acting like they're invisible.

They stop waiting to be moved again.

They start making their bed. They start lighting a candle. They start building altars in their hearts.

Because the sacraments are not about control. They are not rituals to tame the wildness out of a child.

They are about **communion**.

And communion is the one thing every child has always deserved, even if the world forgot to give it.

Now, at last, they get to receive it.

And they don't just receive it once.

They live in it.

They grow in it.

They become it.

Because the sacrament **is** the system.

Chapter Ten

From One House to a Holy Movement

I never set out to build an empire.

I didn't sit down one day and draw up a five-year plan to launch a national initiative or birth a sweeping reformation in the child welfare system. That's not how this started. That's not what I wanted.

I just wanted one house.

One home where a child could feel safe.

One family that wouldn't give up.

One church that actually lived like the Gospel had something to say to children in pain.

That was enough. That was all I could see at first. One home, with a light in the window and the smell of dinner cooking and the sound of prayer rising from the living room. A place where the chaos could be interrupted by beauty, where someone would notice if you were missing.

But holiness doesn't stay small.

It doesn't stay contained.

It spreads like fire. It ignites hearts. It stirs the imaginations of people who thought they were done hoping. And when it touches something real—when it begins to heal souls, raise saints, feed the hungry, restore dignity, and break the back of generational despair—it doesn't remain a single effort. It doesn't stay a private dream.

It becomes a movement.

That's what the Father Flanagan House is becoming. Slowly. Sacramentally. One act of mercy at a time.

Not just a home.

Not just a neighborhood.

A movement of sacred resistance to a system that gave up on children.

A restoration of the Church's forgotten mission.

Phase One: Planting the Prototype

We begin, as all holy things do, with something small and real: the first house.

Not a facility. Not a warehouse for bodies. Not a program with an exit strategy. A home.

We pour everything into this one place. We learn from it. We sit with the kids and listen to what's working and what's not. We listen to the foster parents when they cry. We document everything. Not to scale it for profit—but to preserve the pattern.

We create the formation model: how to raise up foster parents like missionaries. How to train staff not just in trauma, but in spiritual warfare. How to craft a daily rhythm that feeds the soul and regulates the nervous system. How to live liturgically in the middle of crisis.

This house becomes a seed.

And like all good seeds, it carries within it the blueprint for something far greater than itself.

Not a copy. A legacy.

Phase Two: Building the Sacred Neighborhood

The next step is expansion. But not the kind of expansion the world admires.

We're not building out for fame. We're building **in**—for presence.

We add more homes. One, then two. Then five. Then seven. All centered around the sacred: a chapel where prayer never stops. A small parish school where kids are taught with compassion and rigor. A garden where they dig and plant and learn what it means to wait. A gym where bodies can be strengthened and trauma can be released without violence.

We do not build a campus.

We build a **neighborhood**.

A living, breathing parish of mercy.

Each home is not just licensed by the state but consecrated by prayer. The parents are formed not as employees but as shepherds. Every adult in the block is taught the Rule of Life. The daily rhythm of morning prayer, work, study, rest, confession, and Eucharist becomes the scaffolding of every soul on the street.

And then something remarkable happens.

The neighborhood stops being a mission field and starts becoming a **mission force**.

The surrounding community steps in.

Retired couples begin offering respite care on weekends.

Youth groups adopt houses and commit to praying for the children inside them by name.

Knights of Columbus members help with construction and home repairs.

Nuns offer tutoring and counseling. Grandmothers start baking again and show up with casseroles when a new child moves in. The parish stops being a Sunday appointment and starts becoming the pulse of the entire district.

Lines blur.

It becomes harder to tell where the foster care ends and the Church begins.

Because they're the same thing now.

Phase Three: Forming a Rule of Life

Once the sacred neighborhood is established and alive, we write down the Rule.

Not a policy manual. Not a legal binder.

A Rule of Life.

A spiritual constitution drawn from the wisdom of the monastics and the fire of the saints. A rhythm of prayer, meals, work, worship, rest, and reconciliation. We draw from St. Benedict's order, the Irish mission of Celtic Christianity, the joy of the Franciscans, and the fierce mercy of Father Flanagan himself.

We codify not just what we do—but **who we are**.

Each new house, each new team, each new effort takes up this Rule—not as a corporate structure, but as a path to holiness. A way of living that's been tested by fire. A way of walking together that honors suffering, cultivates joy, and refuses to give up on grace.

We're not franchising.

We're founding.

Phase Four: Launching the School of the Saints

As the neighborhood matures, the next step is education—not only for children, but for the adults called into this sacred labor.

We launch a school.

But not a school in the traditional sense. Not just a building with whiteboards and bells.

This is a training ground for spiritual parents, trauma-informed pastors, counselors, caseworkers, mentors, house managers, lay leaders, and teachers.

It's a school where you don't just learn trauma science—you learn **sanctification**.

Where you don't just study case management—you study the art of listening with the ears of Christ.

We teach people how to read files—but more importantly, how to read souls.

It becomes a kind of seminary for the laity. A vocational firepit, where someone who never thought they could do this kind of work begins to realize they were born for it.

They begin to see that God has been preparing them all along.

Phase Five: Sending Out and Starting Over

Eventually, the call comes: go.

A new city. A new state. A new country. A new cluster of children crying out in the darkness.

And when that moment comes, we send.

We lay hands on our staff and volunteers. We anoint our foster parents and chaplains. We send them out not as experts, but as missionaries. They don't go alone. They go with the Rule. They go with the rhythm. They go with the story of what God has done here—and the permission to translate it to the soil where they now labor.

We don't replicate culture.

We **incarnate** it.

We don't copy-paste.

We **translate**.

Every neighborhood looks a little different. But the core is always the same.

A home.

A church.

A rhythm.

A name.

That's the vision. That's the mission.

Not scale. Not platform. Not institutional influence.

But a **quiet revolution of mercy**.

A sacred invasion into the places that have forgotten what a family looks like.

Because we cannot wait for the system to fix itself.

We cannot keep sitting in conferences hoping policy will save the day.

We cannot place our hope in boards, grants, or quarterly funding renewals.

We are the Church.

We are the ones who still believe that every child is made in the image of God.

We are the ones who believe that Jesus meant it when He said, "Whatever you do to the least of these, you do to me."

And we are the ones who will build homes to prove it.

Sacramental homes. Prayerful homes. Unbreakable homes.

Homes that teach a child how to breathe again.

Homes that give them a table and a name.

Homes that raise up saints.

One house at a time.

One neighborhood at a time.

Until the world no longer runs on systems of despair, but sings with the sound of bells ringing in chapels that were once abandoned.

Until every child has a place at the table.

Until every street corner smells like bread and incense.

Until the whole world begins to look—not like an institution—but like the Kingdom of God.

Chapter Eleven

The Return of the Fathers

The crisis we face in child welfare today runs far deeper than a shortage of funding or the failure of policies and bureaucracies. It is not merely a problem of systems, or paperwork, or budgets. At its core, it is a crisis of fatherhood.

Look at the children who come into our care. The overwhelming majority are fatherless—not only in the biological or legal sense but in the spiritual sense. Many of these children have fathers who abandoned them, who disappeared into addiction or violence. Others have fathers who were physically present but emotionally absent—silent bystanders to pain, neglect, or abuse. And some have fathers who actively harmed them, leaving scars that no therapist or caseworker can fully erase.

Where are the men?

Where are the fathers?

I don't mean just men with sperm on file or signatures on a birth certificate. I mean spiritual fathers. Men who show up not just to fill a role on paper, but to embody the sacrificial love that every child desperately needs.

Where are the men who don't run when a child throws a chair across the room but stay and hold the line?

Where are the men who teach discipline with tenderness, who lead family prayers without shame, who build homes not just with their hands but with their hearts?

The truth is, we have outsourced fatherhood.

We've passed the baton to probation officers and therapists.

We've feminized compassion—making caregiving seem like "women's work."

And at the same time, we've demonized strength—branding it as toxic, aggressive, or controlling.

In doing so, we've created a generation of boys who don't know what a holy man looks like. Who don't recognize strength paired with mercy. Who have no model for what it means to be a father who is both a protector and a guide.

It is time to bring these fathers back.

The Knights of Saint George

In response to this crisis, we are raising up a new kind of men's movement.

This is not a club. It is not a casual fellowship.

It is a brotherhood forged in faith and sacrifice.

It is not about machismo or bravado.

It is about Christlike courage.

We call them the Knights of Saint George.

They are not all biological fathers. Many are single men. Some are celibate. Some are wrestling with their own addictions, wounds, and past failures. But all are training—prayerfully, rigorously, and humbly—to become spiritual fathers to children who need them desperately.

Saint George was far more than a dragon slayer in legend.

He was a protector.

A soldier who stood between the vulnerable and violence.

A martyr who refused to betray Christ, even under the most brutal torture.

We are forming men like that.

Men who train their bodies in jiu-jitsu and their souls in daily prayer.

Men unafraid to kneel before the altar or shed tears in confession.

Men who stay up all night beside a boy who's sobbing in the dark.

Men who believe real strength is measured not by domination but by sacrifice.

We teach them to:

- Pray the Divine Office together, morning and night, grounding their day in the presence of God.
- Fast and intercede for the healing of the children in their care, embracing sacrifice as a spiritual weapon.
- Train like athletes because a tired body is a calm body, helping them cultivate discipline and resilience.
- Lead evening Rosaries with their foster sons, cultivating a shared rhythm of prayer and trust.
- Speak blessings over children daily, declaring their dignity and worth aloud.
- Carry the Eucharist into battle—both spiritually and literally—bearing Christ's presence as their shield.

Every Knight of Saint George commits to a rigorous Rule of Life that shapes their identity and mission:

- Daily prayer to center their souls in grace.

- Weekly physical and spiritual training to build strength and humility.
- Monthly spiritual direction to deepen self-awareness and accountability.
- Radical, unwavering support of a foster family or home, making presence their first priority.
- A solemn vow to defend the sacredness of every child as if their very life depended on it.

These men are spiritual bodyguards, intercessors, builders, and priests in the domestic church.

And when the trauma overwhelms—when a boy lashes out in anger or a girl sinks into despair—they do not flee.

They stay.

Because that's what fathers do.

Restoring the Face of the Father

Most children who enter the foster care system have been robbed of the ability to trust a man.

This is not a small or simple wound.

It is cosmic.

Because when a child loses the face of the earthly father, it becomes nearly impossible to trust the face of the Heavenly Father.

The absence of fatherhood distorts a child's view of love, protection, strength, and mercy.

It leaves them vulnerable to fear, shame, and rejection.

The mission before us, then, is not merely emotional support or crisis intervention.

It is sacramental repair.

Each act of presence, patience, and protection is a sacred stitch in the torn fabric of the child's soul.

Each moment of steadfastness rebuilds their capacity to believe in love that stays.

In strength that protects rather than harms.

In power that serves rather than dominates.

And when a boy who once trembled at the sight of a man finally looks a Knight in the eye and says, "I trust you," that is no small thing.

That is a miracle.

That is resurrection.

More Than Mentors: Raising Fathers

We are not merely raising mentors.

We are raising fathers.

Not just creating programs.

We are reclaiming the masculine heart of God.

Because the Father is the original image of strength and tenderness intertwined.

When men return to the sanctuary, children return to hope.

When fathers kneel in prayer, the enemy flees.

This movement is the return of the fathers—not just to homes or families—but to the very sanctuary of the Church.

To reclaim their sacred role as protectors, teachers, and witnesses of God's mercy.

The return of men who will not abandon their children.

Who will fight—not with violence—but with prayer, presence, and sacrifice.

Who will love not with control, but with freedom.

Who will form saints.

Because in the end, the crisis in child welfare is a call—a call to fathers to rise.

To stand in the gap.

To be the face of God's love for children who have nowhere else to turn.

And the time to answer that call is now.

The Path Forward

This is not an easy path.

The wounds we confront are deep and old.

The work is hard and holy.

It demands courage, humility, and endurance.

But it also promises resurrection.

The restoration of broken lives.

The rebirth of hope.

The return of fatherhood.

Because when men rise to their vocation as spiritual fathers, they do not just change one life—they change generations.

They become living bridges between the lost and the Kingdom of God.

They become the embodiment of a Father's heart.

And the Church is renewed.

The family is restored.

The children flourish.

This is the return of the fathers.

And it is the hope for a broken world.

Chapter Twelve

Keeping Time with God

The first thing you lose in trauma is your sense of time.

A child who has been abused, neglected, or uprooted from everything familiar doesn't know what day it is. They don't know when their next meal will come, whether their mom will show up, or when they'll be moved again. Time, for them, becomes a terrifying and unpredictable enemy—unstable, uncontrollable, a relentless reminder that nothing is certain or safe.

This loss of temporal stability is profound because time is more than just minutes and hours. Time is the structure that holds our lives together. It is the rhythm by which we measure hope and expectation. When a child's sense of time shatters, so does their trust in the future.

That's why healing begins with rhythm.

But not just any rhythm.

Sacred rhythm.

At the Father Flanagan House, we don't merely mark time by clocks or calendars. We keep liturgical time. We live by the Church's calendar, the rhythm of feast days and fasts, seasons of joy and sorrow. We order our days, our weeks, our months, and our hearts around the life of Christ.

Because when a child enters into God's time, they begin to discover they are part of something infinitely larger—a story that has order, meaning, beauty, and above all, hope.

Advent: The Season of Waiting

We begin with longing.

Advent is the season of waiting, and waiting is something many traumatized children have never been taught to do.

The first lesson we teach every child is this: It's okay to wait.

You don't have to fix everything right now. You don't have to be okay by next week, or even next month. Healing is a slow work. God came into the world slowly, quietly, through a mother's womb, not with a bang but with a whisper.

So during Advent, we dim the lights, lighting one candle at a time on the wreath.   We sing "O Come, O Come Emmanuel" in hushed, reverent tones. We talk about waiting—not just for Christmas, but for healing, for answers, for love.

We remind them gently, again and again: God always comes.

This lesson in patience becomes a cornerstone for many. They begin to see that waiting is not passive. It is hopeful. It is active trust.

Christmas: The Season of Presence

For many children in care, Christmas is not a joyful celebration. It is a painful reminder of what has been lost—family, security, belonging.

So we reframe the season.

We resist the consumerism and the noise. We don't overdo gifts or cheap thrills. Instead, we focus on presence. On Emmanuel —God with us.

We remind the children that Christ was born into poverty, confusion, and a broken family. They are not far from the manger. They are right there with Him.

On Christmas Eve, we gather in the chapel. We light the final candle on the Advent wreath and proclaim, "Unto us a child is born." Every child hears their name in that line, as if the promise of hope and new life belongs personally to them.

The light in the chapel reflects on their faces—faces that have often known only darkness—and something begins to shift.

Lent: The Season of Repentance

Lent is the season where we get honest.

It is a time to confront wounds, confess sins, and face suffering.

We don't fast to punish ourselves. We fast to walk with Jesus through the desert—a desert familiar to many children who have known abandonment, hunger, and loneliness.

We walk with them.

Together we give up something—a favorite snack, a distraction, a bad habit.

We create space for silence, reflection, and sorrow.

We write down our sins and fears and burn them at the foot of the cross.

And slowly, we teach them that the desert is not the end of the story.

The desert leads to resurrection.

Holy Week: The Week of Truth

Holy Week is the heart of the story.

On Holy Thursday, we wash the feet of the children. Staff, parents, volunteers—one by one, we kneel and pour water over feet that have run from police, kicked through drywall, or walked countless miles in fear.

We say, "You are worth serving."

On Good Friday, we refuse to hide the pain. We name it.

We hold a solemn service for all the losses—parents who never returned, siblings separated, wounds still raw.

We let the children grieve openly.

And on the Easter Vigil, we proclaim what many thought impossible: Love has defeated death.

The darkness gives way to light.

The nightmare ends in joy.

Easter: The Season of Joy

Easter is where joy returns.

Not the fake, superficial kind, but real, messy, loud joy.

The kind that sings at the top of their lungs.

That runs barefoot in the yard.

That eats pancakes after Mass and dances in the living room.

We stretch Easter over 50 days, teaching the children to celebrate—to savor joy as an act of resistance.

Because joy is not a sin.

Joy is a proclamation that darkness does not win.

Pentecost: The Season of Fire

At Pentecost, we anoint the children.

We call down the Spirit.

We remind every teenager that they are part of a mission.

They are not just healing; they are being sent.

We tell them they will one day be the ones to build houses like this, to serve others, to proclaim mercy.

We fan the flame within them.

Because the world told them they were burdens.

Pentecost says, "You are power."

Ordinary Time: The Season of Stability

Then comes Ordinary Time—the long, quiet stretch of green on the Church calendar.

This season is where the daily rhythm settles in: Mass, meals, chores, play, prayer.

It is where children begin to trust.

Where they realize that a normal day can be safe.

Where they learn that ordinary is beautiful.

Where healing grows steady like grass.

Sanctifying Time, Healing Lives

This is how we sanctify time.

Not by piling on more activities.

But by living in rhythm with the mystery of God.

The liturgical year becomes the calendar of healing.

The saints become mentors and companions.

The children who once counted their days in court documents or police reports now count days until Christmas, Easter, or the Feast of St. Joseph.

Because they are not just part of a program anymore.

They are part of a story.

God's story.

And in that story, they are not forgotten.

They are chosen.

The Gift of Sacred Rhythm

Rhythm gives children what trauma took away: stability, predictability, and hope.

When a child learns to keep time with God's calendar, they learn to keep time with their own hearts.

They learn that life has a sacred order.
They discover that they belong.

And when the world outside feels chaotic, the beat of the Church's seasons becomes a steady drum in their souls.

A drum that says: You are held. You are loved. You are part of something eternal.

That is the healing power of sacred time.

That is the healing rhythm of God.

And that is the heartbeat of the Father Flanagan House.

Chapter Thirteen

The Gospel of the Wounded

If you're going to walk into a house like ours, you'd better bring more than good intentions. You'd better bring a theology of the Cross.

Because this work is not clean.

It's not polished or Instagrammable. It's not easy to explain at dinner parties. It's messy, unpredictable, and sometimes shattering. The children we serve carry wounds that don't disappear with medication or motivational speeches. Their pain is too deep, too embedded. It can't be erased or circumvented. It must be carried through, carried alongside, carried with.

And if you don't know how to suffer—how to enter into suffering without running away—you won't last here.

So from the very beginning, we teach it: The Cross is not a decoration. It is a map. A roadmap to redemption. A guide through the dark valleys of pain into the light of resurrection.

Suffering Is Not the Enemy

In the modern child welfare system, the primary goal is often comfort. To quiet the chaos. To reduce risk. To get children "back to normal" as quickly as possible.

But what if there is no normal?

What if the child's trauma cannot be swept under the rug or anesthetized?

What if the child doesn't need to be numbed, but accompanied?

We refuse to send kids the message: "Move on."

Instead, we teach them to move *with* God.

We point them to Jesus—beaten, mocked, abandoned, bleeding—and we say, "He knows your pain."

Not just because He is God, but because He chose to suffer.

He did not avoid pain. He entered it fully, freely, and in doing so, made suffering holy.

The Gospel is not a promise of painlessness. It is a promise of God's presence in pain.

We Don't Fix. We Stay.

There was a boy who couldn't stop punching walls. Every time he felt even the slightest rejection, he would explode. For months, staff tried to manage his behavior. They tried consequences, distractions, and time-outs.

Nothing worked.

One of our foster fathers, worn down but patient, said simply, "Next time it happens, don't run. Just sit with him."

So the next time the boy's anger erupted, the staff member sat quietly on the floor beside him.

Didn't say a word.

Didn't try to fix or fixate.

Just sat.

And waited.

Silently, the boy raged and cried and eventually collapsed into the lap of someone who didn't leave.

That is theology in practice.

That is *kenosis*—the self-emptying love of Christ poured out, not in flashy words or heroic acts, but in humble, steadfast presence.

We don't fix.

We stay.

The Stations of Their Cross

Every child who comes through our doors has a Passion narrative—a journey of suffering that mirrors, in many ways, the Stations of the Cross:

- Taken from the home they know.
- Betrayed by those they trusted most.
- Judged by strangers who know nothing of their story.
- Labeled with words that wound: "defiant," "damaged," "lost."
- Shuffled through placements like a piece on a board.
- Mocked and misunderstood by peers and adults alike.
- Abandoned, forgotten, left to fend for themselves.
- Stripped of dignity and hope.
- Left to die slowly in the cold machinery of the system.

We walk with them through each station.

We do not rush to Easter.

We do not pretend the pain isn't real or deep.

We hold their hand through Good Friday—the darkest day.

And slowly—sometimes painfully—they begin to believe that they have a Companion on this journey. That their suffering is not meaningless. That maybe, just maybe, God has not forgotten them.

Resurrection Takes Time

We do not promise quick fixes or fairy-tale endings.

We don't parade success stories like trophies.

We plant seeds.

We nurture roots.

Sometimes, we never get to see the harvest.

Sometimes, the child leaves and never calls again.

But sometimes—five, ten, even fifteen years later—we receive a letter.

"I'm sober now."

"I forgave my mom."

"I'm going to school."

"I'm getting married."

Those are resurrection moments.

They come slowly.

Quietly.

Often long after we have given up hope.

But they come.

Because the tomb is not the end.

And neither is the trauma.

Healing is a journey—a pilgrimage that requires patience, faith, and unyielding love.

God's Wounds Heal Our Own

Father Solanus Casey used to say, "Thank God ahead of time."

That's how we live.

We thank God ahead of time for the healing we haven't yet seen.

For the miracle buried deep inside the meltdown.

For the grace hidden within the grief.

We teach the children to offer their pain—not in despair—but as a prayer.

"Jesus, use this."

"Make this matter."

When children learn to pray from the depths of their wounds, they become something the world rarely understands:

Prophets.

They speak truth—not only about trauma and broken systems, but about God Himself—the God who entered into human pain and never wastes it.

We Do Not Romanticize Suffering, But We Do Not Run From It

We do not paint suffering with a rosy brush.

We do not glorify brokenness.

But neither do we avoid it.

We walk through suffering, slowly and together.

Hand in hand, step by step.

Because the Gospel is not a promise to avoid pain.

It is a promise to redeem it.

Every time we walk a child through their own Passion.

Every time we help carry their Cross.

We live out the profound mystery of Christ's love.

This is the theology of our house.

This is the Gospel of the wounded.

This is the only kind of hope worth building a neighborhood for.

A hope that is real.

A hope that suffers.

A hope that conquers.

Because in the brokenness, God is at work.

And that is the gospel worth living for.

Chapter Fourteen

The Church Must Rise

There is no one else coming.

No next wave of better social workers, no miracle government programs with endless funding, no secret philanthropist waiting to unveil a flawless model.

If the Church does not rise, these children will fall.

And for far too long, we have pretended this crisis belongs to someone else.

We have treated child homelessness like a mere social issue, foster care as just another government responsibility, and the Church as a place of sacraments disconnected from suffering. We have compartmentalized mercy and worship, forgetting that they are meant to be inseparable.

But the early Church never worked that way.

The early Church didn't petition Rome to care for orphans.

They *adopted* them.

They took children off the streets—the ones left to die in the cold, the ones society labeled "unfit," "illegitimate," or simply invisible—and they gave them homes. Not programs. Homes.

They didn't wait for permission or fill out endless forms.

They acted immediately, because their theology demanded it.

Their faith called them to embody the mercy of Christ in concrete ways.

Your Parish Is a Shelter

Every parish has empty rooms.

Every rectory has extra space.

Every parish hall could host a support group, a meal program, a laundry service, or a small bedroom for a young person aging out of foster care with nowhere else to turn.

This is not some idealistic dream. It is doable.

But we need more than good intentions.

We need a *new ecclesiology*—a renewed vision of what the Church *is* and *must be*.

The Church is not merely the guardian of sacraments and doctrines.

She is the *mother* of orphans.

She is the refuge of the vulnerable.

She is the home of the homeless.

She is the sanctuary where the forgotten find their name again.

We should be known for this.

When someone says "Catholic," they should immediately think:

"Oh, those are the ones who take in the kids."

Not just the pro-life ones at the voting booth.

The whole-life ones.

The ones who raise children, feed them, heal their wounds, confirm them, walk them down the aisle on their wedding day, and bury them with dignity.

This is the Church's calling.

To embody the Gospel not just in word, but in deed.

Every Diocese Needs a Sacred Neighborhood

We've proven it can be done—one house at a time.

Now, we need bishops and diocesan leaders to act decisively.

Not just to write statements or call for awareness.

But to allocate resources—land, buildings, personnel.

To reimagine unused convents, shuttered schools, and empty properties—not as liabilities, but as sacred opportunities.

To build not more chancery offices or administrative suites, but *sacred neighborhoods.*

Liturgical homes.

Eucharistic communities formed to cradle traumatized children and the families who care for them.

These neighborhoods are not charity projects.

They are incarnations of the Body of Christ.

They are the Church living and breathing.

We need dioceses to:

- Invest in training spiritual foster families, not just caregivers.
- Recruit retired clergy to become chaplains to trauma-formed communities, offering daily prayer, confession, and pastoral presence.
- Restore sacramental imagination as the core of healing, not an afterthought.
- Collaborate with religious orders and lay ministries to staff, sustain, and evangelize these neighborhoods.

This is not an optional add-on.

It is the essential mission of the Church in our broken world.

The Religious Orders Must Return to the Margins

Mother Frances Xavier Cabrini did not build hospitals to add lines to her resume.

She built them because no one else would.

Religious orders have always been called to *go where no one else will go.*

The streets.

The docks.

The prisons.

The leper colonies.

The mines.

The orphanages.

And today, that call is to the margins of foster care, to the children who have been discarded by society.

These children are the ones everyone wants to avoid, control, or forget.

We need sisters, brothers, monks, and friars to answer the call again.

To live among these children.

To pray over them.

To love them into sainthood.

This is not a distraction from the spiritual life.

It *is* the spiritual life.

It is the work of mercy incarnate.

It is the Church in its most radical, vulnerable, and beautiful form.

Lay People: You Are the Front Line

You don't need permission.

If you have a house, open it.

If you have a room, fill it.

If you have love, give it.

You don't need to be perfect.

You don't need a degree or a certificate.

You need willingness.

The Lord will do the rest.

The saints were laypeople, too.

They took risks.

They were misunderstood.

They made mistakes.

And then, they changed the world.

You can do the same.

Your home can be a sanctuary.

Your hands can be instruments of healing.

Your prayers can sustain a community.

We Are Not Asking the Church to Become Something New

We are asking her to become what she *always* was.

A refuge.

A table.

A home.

A place where Christ is present not only on the altar but also in the child who walks through the door shaking—unsure if they will be loved.

It's time.

We cannot outsource holiness.

We cannot delegate mercy.

The Church must rise.

Because if she doesn't—

Then what, exactly, is she for?

The Church's Urgent Call

The challenges in child welfare are immense.

Complex social problems layered with historical neglect and systemic failure.

But none of those excuses can deter the Church from her mission.

When the Gospel calls us to care for the orphan, the widow, the stranger, it is not an invitation to committee meetings or social media campaigns.

It is a summons to *action*.

To live out our faith with radical generosity.

To become the hands and feet of Christ in a world that desperately needs Him.

The time to wait is over.

The time to pray silently is past.

The time to rise is now.

From Parishes to Neighborhoods, from Neighborhoods to Cities

Imagine every parish becoming a shelter.

Every parish hall a refuge.

Every clergy house a home for those in need.

Imagine networks of sacred neighborhoods in every diocese.

Communities where trauma-informed care meets the sacraments.

Where foster families are spiritual families.

Where the Church becomes known for her *body* as much as her *baptismal* identity.

Where the poor, the broken, the wounded, and the forgotten find not just programs, but belonging.

This is not a pipe dream.

It is the Church's destiny.

It is the vision we must claim.

Your Part in the Story

You don't have to be a bishop or a religious sister.

You don't have to have years of training or a public platform.

You just have to say yes.

Yes to opening your home.

Yes to loving a child who might not look like you or speak your language.

Yes to standing in the gap where the world has turned away.

Yes to the Church's call to holiness, mercy, and radical love.

The future of the Church depends on it.

The future of these children depends on it.

And God is calling you—right now—to rise.

This is the hour.

The Church must rise.

Because in the rising, the lost are found.

In the rising, the forgotten are remembered.

In the rising, the Kingdom of God begins to break through.

Will you answer the call?

Chapter Fifteen

The Monastery for the Modern Age

I used to think monasteries were relics.

Beautiful, yes. Historic. Inspiring.

But distant. Disconnected. Places reserved for the ultra-holy, the ultra-quiet, or the ultra-retired.

Places removed from the noise, the mess, and the heartbreak of the world.

I thought monasteries were something of the past—a spiritual luxury in a time when faith was simpler, slower, and somehow less complicated.

Then I started working with traumatized children.

Then I saw what chaos does to the soul.

I saw how trauma tears apart the fabric of a child's inner life—not just emotionally or psychologically, but physically and spiritually.

I saw how the very sense of time, safety, belonging, and self can be shattered beyond recognition.

And then I understood why the Church, in her ancient wisdom, built monasteries and cloisters and religious communities where life was ordered, prayerful, anchored, and sheltering.

Because what trauma destroys—monasteries rebuild.

What trauma scatters—monasteries gather.

What trauma breaks—monasteries repair.

And now, I believe: the only way forward is back.

Not back to isolation or withdrawal from the world.

But back to *structure*.

Not back to escaping reality.

But back to *sanctuary within it*.

A Different Kind of Monastery

We are building what I call the *Monastery for the Modern Age*.

It has habits and holy hours—but also soccer games, therapy sessions, kitchen table confessions, and messy family dinners.

It has quiet cells for silence—and couches for chaos.

It's a monastery where kids can scream, cry, and rage—and someone will still kneel beside them without fear or frustration.

Where the bells ring not only for Lauds and Vespers, but also for family dinner, bedtime prayers, and Sunday Mass held in a school gym.

It is a place where the *Divine Office* meets the *messy office of social care*.

A place where liturgy is not an escape from trauma—it is the *pattern that heals* it.

What It Looks Like

At the center is always a chapel.

The Eucharist is present—continually.

Candles burn day and night, flickering softly in the dim light.

Someone is always praying—either silently or aloud.

Around the chapel: homes. Real homes.

With bedrooms and porches. Gardens and pets.

Each home belongs to a family—trained, formed, and vowed to the mission of hospitality and healing.

Around the homes: rhythm.

- Morning prayer at seven o'clock, waking the soul with praise.
- Breakfast together, a communal moment to begin the day.
- Work and school, interspersed with laughter and occasional tears.
- Midday Angelus, a pause to remember God's presence in the ordinary.
- Evening Mass or Vespers, a sacred gathering to end the workday.
- Family dinner, the meal of connection, nourishment, and conversation.
- Compline before bed, a time of quiet reflection and rest.

The calendar follows the Church year.

The saints smile from the walls, their lives a testament to grace.

The *Rule of Life* governs everything—not harshly or rigidly, but quietly, lovingly, with clarity and purpose.

It's not just trauma-informed.

It's *glory-informed.*

Who Lives There

- Families called to foster and adopt, living the Gospel in flesh and blood.
- Staff committed not only to casework but to *long-term spiritual formation.*
- Volunteers living out lay consecration, offering their time and talents to the community.

- Former foster youth who now want to stay—to give back what they have received.
- Priests who pray, anoint, teach, and listen, weaving sacrament into every moment.
- Religious sisters who mentor and intercede, embodying mercy and steadfastness.
- Children—broken, holy, and learning to live again.

This is not a facility.

It is not a commune.

It is not merely a shelter.

It is a *village of saints-in-the-making*.

And every person who enters—whether for an hour or a lifetime—knows this:

God lives here.

Why It Works

Because most foster care environments are chaotic.

Because trauma is stored in the body, not just the mind.

Because trauma is caused by disordered rhythms, ruptured attachments, and a total lack of spiritual safety.

A monastery heals this by:

- Giving structure to time, allowing children to find stability in the predictable.
- Giving reverence to the body, teaching respect for oneself and others.
- Giving space for silence, inviting reflection and restoration.
- Giving meaning to suffering, showing that pain can be transformed.

- Giving God back to the center, restoring the soul's true home.

This isn't just about better care.

It's about *eternal care*.

It's about restoring *worship* to the wounded.

It's about building a *sanctuary* where the sacred and the broken meet.

Why It's Urgent

Because the culture is not getting calmer.

Because boys and girls are being raised in homes without prayer.

Because teens are drowning in screens and loneliness.

Because children are dying in foster care—alone, unheard, and unseen.

We cannot wait for the perfect model.

We cannot wait for more funding, better policies, or ideal conditions.

We have to build now.

A monastery in the neighborhood.

A chapel in the storm.

A house where God is not just spoken of, but experienced.

The Dream

The dream is that every child will have a home not just for their body but for their soul.

That every child will find rhythm and refuge, prayer and play, love and liturgy.

That every community will be a monastery in miniature.

A place where chaos is met with calm.

Where suffering is met with hope.

Where the wounds of the past are not ignored, but healed through grace.

The Call

This is the call.

Not just to the religious or the trained professional.

But to every Christian.

To every parish.

To every family.

To reclaim the ancient wisdom of monastic life—not as an escape from the world, but as a *sanctuary within it.*

To build spaces where trauma is not simply managed but transformed.

Where children learn not only to survive but to *thrive.*

The monastery for the modern age is more than a place.

It is a way of life.

It is a rhythm of healing.

It is the Church living fully into her mission of sanctifying the broken.

And it begins with a single step.

Will you take it?

Chapter Sixteen

What If We Did It?

Just imagine.

What if we did it?

What if every diocese in this country—and around the world—committed itself to building *one sacred neighborhood* dedicated to healing the wounds of childhood trauma? What if every parish, no matter how small, took *one foster child* seriously—not just in word, but in tangible, life-changing action? What if every religious order reclaimed its ancient mission and adopted a block of abandoned homes, restoring them as monasteries for the modern world—a place where saints are made amid the broken?

What if we stopped asking what's *realistic*, what's *possible* by worldly standards—and started asking what's *holy*?

What if we finally dared to live the Gospel not just as a beautiful idea, but as a fierce, uncompromising reality?

Imagine the Children

Imagine the ones sleeping tonight in the cramped offices of social workers, the kids shuffled between hospital beds and foster homes, whose only certainty is uncertainty.

What if next year, instead of cold floors and fluorescent lights, those same children were sleeping in homes where the Psalms were sung softly over them at bedtime? Where their names were spoken in prayer, where their hurts were carried not just by therapists but by families who *believed* in their healing?

Imagine the children labeled "too broken," "too damaged," "too lost" by a system that writes them off before giving them a chance.

What if those children were instead being *confirmed* in their faith, serving at the altar, learning to pray the Rosary, and cooking dinner with spiritual fathers and mothers who refused to give up on them?

Imagine the girl who has been moved twenty-six times in five years—what if she finally had a *room of her own,* a place to hang her clothes, a small sanctuary where she could kneel, cry, and know for the first time that she was *safe*?

What if the teenage boy who only knows abandonment walked into a home with a crucifix on the wall and someone said to him with absolute certainty, "This is the house of God—and it's your house now"?

What if they knew, for the very first time, that they were not invisible? That they were not a burden. That they were *chosen.*

Imagine the Churches

What if our empty convents and shuttered schools were filled again—not with paperwork and bureaucracy, but with the *laughter of children*?

What if our parish halls, instead of being rented out for meetings about finances, smelled like fresh baked bread and echoed with the prayers of Rosaries said for the healing of a hurting child?

What if our Sunday announcements weren't about the latest committee fundraiser or parish social, but instead celebrated the confirmations from the Flanagan House? Celebrated the boy who passed his math test for the first time. Celebrated the young woman who marked her first year sober. Celebrated every small victory that the world overlooks but God delights in?

What if the most devout people in our churches weren't arguing online, but were out in the trenches—cooking meals for traumatized kids, cleaning bathrooms in sacred homes, sitting patiently through long nights of tears and prayers?

What if holiness wasn't something preached from a pulpit but was *embodied* in every act of mercy, every meal served, every wound tended?

What if the Church became known as the place where *hope* is born again?

Imagine the Future Saints

What if the next Saint Francis of Assisi came not from privilege or safety but from foster care?

What if the next Mother Cabrini was a girl abandoned at birth, found by a praying woman, raised in a home where she learned to love God before she could read?

What if the next Father Solanus Casey was a quiet boy who stuttered, overlooked by the world, but who found peace kneeling night after night before the Eucharist?

What if the next Father Flanagan is already here—but he's sitting in a group home right now, angry, lonely, convinced no one sees him?

What if the saints of the next century will not come from seminaries or religious orders alone—but from the very children we refuse to abandon today?

We don't need to wait 100 years to see new saints born.

We just have to build the *house* where they can grow.

This Is the Time

The world is aching.

Our systems are fracturing under the weight of trauma and neglect.

Our children are hurting in ways we barely understand.

But the Church—if she wakes up—can be more than a mere remnant, more than a fading institution weighed down by bureaucracy and scandal.

She can be a *revolution of mercy*.

She can be a network of *holy homes*—each one a sanctuary, a beacon of light in the darkness.

She can be the ark that carries these children safely through the floodwaters of despair into the promised land of healing and hope.

And when we look back decades from now, we will say:

That was the moment.

That was the turning.

That was the year the Church remembered who she was— and made every orphan feel *wanted* again.

We Don't Need a Better Plan

We don't need another blueprint from social work experts.

We don't need more studies or committees.

What we need is to *believe again*.

Believe in the sacraments—not as symbols, but as life-giving encounters.

Believe in the saints—not as distant heroes, but as present examples of grace transforming broken lives.

Believe in *each other*—not as strangers or clients, but as brothers and sisters in Christ.

And most of all—

Believe in the God who said,

"Whatever you do for the least of these, you do unto me."

We've seen His face.

And it was covered in tears.

Now We Will Build the House

We will open the doors.

We will set the table.

We will prepare the beds.

We will kneel beside every broken child and say,

"You are home."

We will stay when it's hard.

We will hold on when hope feels distant.

We will love without conditions, without limits, without quitting.

Because this is not just charity.

This is not just social work.

This is *the Church*.

This is *the Body of Christ*.

And every child is a living member.

And We Will Never Leave

Not until every child is home.

Not until every child knows they belong.

Not until every child has a family.

Not until every child is *loved*.

This is our mission.

Our promise.

Our sacred call.

The Gospel in action.

The Kingdom breaking in.

The Church rising up.

What if we did it?

What if we said yes?

What if we became the answer the world has been praying for?

It's not too late.

The time is now.

The Church is ready.

The children are waiting.

Will you answer the call?

If we do it—if we dare to love this deeply, to build this boldly, to hold this faithfully—

Then we will change everything.

We will rewrite the story of orphanhood.

We will create neighborhoods where hope is real and healing is possible.

We will birth a new generation of saints.

And the world will see the face of God—reflected in the faces of children finally home.

Let us begin.